WALKING THE ROAD TO RECOVERY!

9 STEPS IN MOTION!
By Michael A. Muhammad

Copyright 2020 Michael A Muhammad

Table of Contents

Preface

It all began with a single question: "When you stopped using drugs, how did you get rid of the craving?" I had to stop and think. Though I have been asked many questions over the years about how I got off drugs, this was a new one. As I pondered the question and shared my experience, the steps that form the basis of this book began to unfold. The following day, I was being interviewed by Joshua Muhammad on the People's Podcast. During the interview, I shared some aspects in my journey to overcome addiction. Then, he asked the question that sealed the deal. He wanted to know if I would be willing to speak with people who had questions regarding addiction. In that moment, I knew it was time for this book.

"The answers to our prayers come through people, places, and things, and time and condition will determine how soon you will receive it." These are the wise words of a beloved friend, elder, and mentor, the late great Brother Milton D. Muhammad. He would keep these words in the forefront of my mind so that I would realize the significant role that the human connection along with the appropriate time and circumstances play in the fulfillment of our prayers. This critical time, where addiction is on the rise, has put me in touch with the importance of bringing what is in my heart and mind to the pages of this book, so that anyone, anywhere, at any time can access it. Just as there were those who were an answer to a prayer for me on the road to recovery, I pray that through this book, I can also be an answer for someone else along the way.

Let's gooooooo!

-Brother Michael A. Muhammad

STEP ONE

MAKE THE DECISION

*"PROGRAM?! I DON'T NEED NO
DAMN PROGRAM!"*

*"HOOKED ON DRUGS?! I JUST BEEN
SMOKING CRACK FOR SIX YEARS!
THAT DON'T MEAN I'M
ADDICTED!"*

*"I CAN STOP USING DRUGS
WHENEVER I PLEASE!"*

*"GETTING HIGH MAKE YOU DEEP! I
LIKE
TO HAVE DEEP CONVERSATIONS,
YOU
KNOW!"*

*"SHI… KILLING ME?! EVERYBODY
GOTTA DIE SOME WAY!*

*"THIS MY LAST HIT! THIS MY LAST
TIME GETTING HIGH!"*

"The Honorable Elijah Muhammad said when people wrote him about their bad habits, "How can I stop?" he said, "Just stop." Why would he say something like that? There's no big, long drawn out thing to break a habit. You have to develop the Will to stop, and then stop! You can stop heroine! You can stop reefer! You can stop drugs! You can stop any bad habit once you make up your mind!"
Quoted from The Restrictive Law of Islam is Our Success
By The Honorable Minister Louis Farrakhan

The mind has to be made up to make the decision. What decision? Do I love life? Do I want to live? If the answer to these questions are yes, then the decision has to be made to not continue to knowingly kill yourself with drugs, cigarettes and alcohol. I mention these three vices for the purpose of this writing. However, there are many ways that we destroy ourselves through addiction. I'm just sharing my testimony as a reference point from which principles can be drawn and applied to any situation involving addictive, self-destructive behavior.

Decision is a conclusion or resolution reached after consideration. In boxing, a decision is the awarding of a fight, in the absence of a knockout or technical knockout, to the boxer with the most rounds won or with the most points. Now, before you knock yourself out of life, make a decision. Here is a quick story. When I was 19 years old, my niece Angel was 3 years old. I had just come into a certain knowledge of the black man's contribution to civilization. I read the autobiography of Malcolm X. I just started going back to church. Not just any church. But, the great Union
Temple Baptist Church under the leadership of
Reverend Willie F. Wilson, who has an Afrocentric theology. So, I am receiving all of this uplifting information. As I am learning, I am teaching my niece. One day I was sitting on the couch smoking a cigarette. My niece hops up on the couch beside me and asks, "Uncle Mike, why do you smoke?" I promise you, I felt terrible.

My thoughts were, what excuse am I going to give to a 3 year old? Then she said, "U know it's killing you, right?" Right then and there I made a decision to never let her see me smoke again. I didn't stop smoking, yet. But, her words kept ringing in my ears every time I lit a cigarette. I spent a few years hiding from little Angel every time I wanted to take a smoke.

After running myself through the fire of this self-imposed hell with lying and stealing and smoking up paycheck after paycheck, it was just a matter of time before I would completely self-destruct. Hanging out on drug strips all through the night in the late 80s and early 90s during a time when the DMV (Washington DC Metropolitan area) had become the murder capital of the country, I saw so much destruction of human life. It was one day in early 1991 that I cashed my paycheck, and from that moment throughout the night I began to smoke up my entire check. At the time I had a "good" government job with FDIC. So, I was "beaming up" all night. I ran out of cash and there was my little cousin's purse sitting there welcoming my thievery. She was staying with us at the time. After emptying her purse, I was down to her bank card. And, I promise you, if I could've figured out her pin code I would've wiped her out. I found one more $20 bill in my mother's coat pocket and took that out to a strip in SE DC called Valley Green. The dope man told me to come in the building. He gave me the crack rock. I gave him the money. I looked at it and knew it was a "dummy." It was fake. But, I am surrounded by known killers. So, I was blessed to get out of that building alive. This dummy move I made was necessary to produce the shift in my thinking that would lead to the decision that would ultimately save my life. Picture this dummy. After blowing my whole check to get high; then emptying my baby cousin's purse, who I am supposed to protect and be a role model. And to top it off, stealing from the woman who struggled as a single parent to sacrifice everything for me, there was nothing in my life more low life and shameful as this feeling. This is what had become my rock bottom. Everyone's rock bottom is not the same.

However, the rock bottom experience is usually what produces the mind to make a decision. A decision must be made.

When you make your decision it has to be for you. When you are addicted to drugs, over time you begin to lose all shame. Even if you are hiding, once you kill the voice of reason on the inside, your outside appearance doesn't even matter. But, when you reach rock bottom and can no longer face yourself in the mirror, you really start changing on the inside. When the disgust of your very existence begin to penetrate your heart, your appearance begin to matter to you. That's what's important. You don't want your decision to be rooted in people pleasing, or how someone else feels about you. People pleasing is another addiction that has the potential to interfere with your growing love for self, to satisfy someone else's desire to control you. Take control of your life and enjoy the journey of making the right decisions.

Make the decision. Decide to change. Affirm in your mind and out of your mouth that it is time to make a change. Then, you can start exploring the true power in the mind to change. It's going to be a challenge. But, we have until the last bell ring before the ultimate decision is made. The decision is made. The journey begins. With love all things are possible

STEP TWO

Finding the Love

As I was drowning in the abyss of self-hate, I was looking for love in all the wrong places. And while I was blasting that pipe, if someone would ask me if I loved myself, my answer would be, "Of course I do. What do you mean, do I love myself? But, I didn't realize that the act of smoking crack is the result of a deep seeded hatred for myself that would produce self-destruction. It was easy for me to say emphatically, yes of course I love myself in the absence of knowing what love really is. So, what is love?

In the dictionary love as a noun is an intense feeling of deep affection. It is a great interest and pleasure in something. As a verb it states, to feel a deep romantic or sexual attachment to (someone). This is very basic and elementary when it comes to a word as powerful as love. Hence, this very shallow definition of love made it easy for me to say and think that I loved myself as I was killing myself. The Honorable Minister Louis Farrakhan teaches that love is force and power. He also said that love is the creative force out of which all things are create. Therefore, where there is love there is life. Love goes beyond feelings and emotions. With this in mind, rational and critical thinking has to be in the equation when it comes to this most misunderstood word called love.

In this step we want to introduce a drill. Most people, if asked, "Do you love yourself?" The answer will immediately come out. "Yes!" If this question is followed by, why? Or, How? You might run into a jam. In this step it is imperative that you take the time to think it through and write down at least 10 reasons why you love yourself. Once you write them out, analyze them. Internalize them. Through these 9 steps to recovery they are going to always come in handy. In fact, you don't have to stop at 10. Write down as many reasons you can think of why you love yourself. Now, let's explore your mind a little bit.

How deep is your love? On a scale of 1-10, 1, being not so often, 10, being very often,

1. How often do you exercise to keep your body in good shape?
2. How often do you consciously make the effort to consume healthy foods and drinks?
3. How often do you feed your mind with something inspirational?
4. How often do you set goals to advance your life?
5. How often do you reward yourself for accomplishments that you may achieve?

When I started my journey to recovery, it was so hard to come up with 10 real reasons why I had love for self that went beyond feelings and emotions. However, once I was able to dig deep through the mud of self-hate, it became so therapeutic to be able to constantly review and feed on the reasons why I could truly say I have love for myself. This is a very important step towards recovery. Since love is force and power, and the creative force from which all things come, the more you grow to love yourself the more you will generate the power to overcome addiction. Consequently, the more you love yourself, the more your actions will become aligned with that which will give you abundant life.

There is another aspect of finding the love. Once you can find love in you it's critical, particularly in the early stages of recovery to align with others who share that love. This adds to the force and power generated. Just like hot coals keep each other lit. Now, you have to be selective with the company you keep to determine whether they will be an asset in the journey to recovery. Or, will my interaction with them keep me on my ass. In other words, will these relationships add to my life? In my case, I first reached out to my mother. When I hit my rock bottom stage I wasn't able to even look at myself in the mirror. It became so evident that I needed some serious help. So, I called my mother and told her point blank, "I am killing myself and don't even care! I need some help." It was something about confessing the truth with someone I love, who I knew loved me. This lifted a burden. Then, I called my aunt who had overcome drug abuse in her past to make that same confession. They both stepped up to the plate to make themselves available for my open and true expression. Another key intervention was my late uncle Paul Armstrong. He did something very significant. He directed me to the Bible in the 7th chapter of Romans. He said, read that and we will talk about what you have read. This was the 1st time that someone took the time to sit with me personally to give me understanding of scripture, where my particular situation was concerned. More on this in a later step. The point here is to find any loved ones who you know have your best interest to allow expression.

Finding the love is so important. Drugs appeal to the pleasure center. There is not a human being on the planet who doesn't want pleasure. This world is set up to drown humanity in the sea of pleasure. And, if our since of self is not on the level it should and could be, the disappointment in self drives us toward the need to escape reality with something pleasurable. There is nothing wrong with seeking pleasure. The problem is in the lack of knowledge of self. The lack of the knowledge of self is dangerous in a world like the world in which we live. Why? Because this world has a lot to offer that goes contrary to our nature. Self-preservation is the first law of nature. I heard the Honorable Minister Louis Farrakhan say that there is nothing about our nature that loves to intake death. Finding true love will help us preserve life. So, find the love. Write it out. You don't have to stop at 10 things. Write as many as you can come up with. Feed on them. Embrace them to the degree that it brightens your very countenance as you start your day in your walk to recovery.

STEP THREE

Out With the Old

TA HA (O Man)

In the name of Allah, the Beneficent, the Merciful O

man,

We have not revealed the Qur'an to thee that thou mayest be unsuccessful.

{Holy Qur'an Surah 20:1&2)

The decision is made. Self-love is being nurtured. The journey begins. Reverend Willie F. Wilson taught that when you get baptized, it's not the end of your journey. In fact, this is where your journey begins. That made a lot of since. Because when he dipped me in that water, trust me, I didn't feel too much different from before I got in the water. The biggest difference is that I was soak-n-wet! He took the mysticism out of the ritual. He also made a profound statement that it took a while for me to embrace and understand. He said, *"You have to pray as if everything depends on God.*

And, work as if everything depends on you." This makes a whole lot of sense to me now. But, in the beginning stages of my walk on this road to recovery I was a little confused. I had to come face to face with the reality that faith without works is dead. This is a step by step and day by day journey. In fact, the mind travels so fast, this is a moment to moment journey. It only takes a split second to change your mind. What is fed to the mind becomes very important. And, what has to be considered is how the mind has already been fed to get caught up in drug abuse. This is why this step is called, "out with the old."

Out with the old. What we would liken this step to is when your computer has so many files, programs, software and so on, that you can't get it to perform to the capacity that it's designed to perform. Or, try moving from a 3 bedroom, 2 level house into a 1 bedroom apartment. It's time to let some things go. Some of those files and programs are making your computer move way too slow. Some of those things that you are trying to hold on to should have never even made it to the house.

So, it's definitely no room for them in the apartment. Same goes with this new person that you are striving to become. Everything can't come with you. Not only does your environment along with the company you keep have to change, the old you has to make way for this new person that's being developed moment to moment.

Let's look at something. There is a lot of time, energy and effort spent to maintain the life of a drug addict. If you have money you can go and make your purchase, use your drug of choice and the journey begins. Then, when you run out of money there is time and energy spent on plotting and scheming. You know how it goes. Once the ball gets rolling, it's a never ending journey. Now you're putting time in hanging around to see who will invite you to their next move. If that's not the case you're looking for ways to rob and steal. What's the point? If all of this comes to a halt because of your decision to quit, then you have a lot of time on your hands. And, you know what they say, *"An idle mind is the devil's playground."* Even though it is necessary to cut back on most of what your daily activity once was, you will stand the chance of being way too idle.

We stated earlier in this writing that drugs appeal to the pleasure center. One of the things to guard yourself against is anything that would feed your lower nature. When you start cleaning up your life there will still be so much temptation around you. It must be understood that for every action there is an equal and opposite reaction. There are so many vices that will test you in the decision that you have made. For instance, we live in a sex crazed world. And, because sex is natural, you can find yourself shifting your addiction to sexual promiscuity if you're not careful. I say this from experience. And, this is just a note of caution to guard yourself against any subtleties that could lead in this direction.

This is also a time where cigarettes and alcohol abuse tend to pick up if that was a part of your routine. Each one of these can lead you right back down the slippery slope. Each one of these habits can trigger the desire to go right back to the drugs. Either that, or they all have the potential to get out of hand and kill you even faster.

Out with the old has everything to do with the way one thinks. How is your thinking? I used to think that it was the company that I kept. So, my thought was, let me stay away from these people who, *"all they want to do is get high."* Guess what I found? I found out that I was the main person I needed to get away from.
Hmmm. That "old me." How in the world am I going to do that? It starts with the thinking.
There is a saying, "Thoughts produce actions. Actions creates habits. And, habits shape character." You have to be conscious of the thoughts traveling through your mind. A total awareness of self is the key. This means that you have to guard

against what your eyes see, what your ears hear and what your heart suggests. In the Holy Qur'an Surah 113, *AlFalaq* The Dawn, it reads,

"In the name of Allah, the Beneficent, the Merciful,

1 *Say; I seek refuge in the Lord of the dawn,*

2 *From the evil of that which He has created.*

3 *And from the evil of intense darkness, when it comes,*

4 *And, from the evil of those who cast (evil suggestions) in firm resolutions,*

5 *And from the evil of the envier when he envies."*

If the old you would hang out in the streets all night until the break of dawn, out with the old. If the old you often looked to rob, cheat and steal to get that next hit, out with the old. If the old you would feed on the darkness of self to see who could be taken advantage of for that next hit, out with the old. If the old you quickly responds to evil suggestions, inward and outward, to feed that dope addict tendency, out with the old. If envy of someone who has what you desire causes you to do them harm and take what you can get from them to feed your addiction, out with the old you. In order to get through this step, be ready to say farewell to the person that you have gotten so use to. Know and understand that the old you will work to bully you around and force you to remain under their control. The old you has gotten real comfortable in your skin. The old you knows that they don't belong in existence any longer. However, they don't intend to leave you alone. In fact, the old you will play on your emotions and ask, "What are you going to do without me?" This is all in the mind. And, you have the power to change your mind.

So, as you are getting rid of that old you and preparing yourself for the brightness of a new day,

1.   Pay close attention to what you allow to feed your mind. What are your triggers? In my battle against drug abuse, being alone with my thoughts thinking of everything that I haven't accomplished, want to accomplish and need to accomplish could bring about a depression that would trigger me to want to get high. Or, watching a movie and seeing something that reminds me of my personal life. Then, all of a sudden, I'm in my feelings about it and ready to make a bad decision.

2.   Pay close attention to how this world makes evil fair seeming. This world is made for addictions to thrive. Whatever indulgences you desire in this world, you can get it in abundance. There is a liquor store on every corner. Acquiring any illegal drug simply is a matter of asking around. Most drug strips are clearly drug strips. City to city and state to state, the drug spots are very identifiable. This is a world where you can win an Oscar for portraying gangsters. You can win a Grammy for music with lyrical content that portrays a degenerate lifestyle. Trap music is just

that; a trap. Some of the most popular movies featured drug lords and thug life. So, the ability to distinguish fantasy from reality becomes very important.

3.   Be honest with yourself as to how easy it is to get dark right along with the darkness of this world. Knowing this makes it imperative to continue to feed on, and continue to build on the self-love that was documented in step two.

4.   Understand that while you are packing the bags of the old you preparing the eviction, remember that you are dealing with a slick person, a thief and robber, a liar and a cheat. So, don't be surprised if you wake up the next morning and that old you ends up right there in the bed with you.

The reality is that this is a part of yourself that must be put in check. Depending on how long you have been under the condition of addiction, it's like a big young man verses an infant. For me it was 14 years. So, imagine a 14 year old's strength over an infant that just got here 90 days ago. So, when you reach 30 days, 60 days,

90 days, continue to shine the light on this new and improved person that is growing in you, and nurture it as if it is a new born infant. You will be successful. This leads me right into the next step. I am prayerful that this is all coming together and making sense. It's time to bring in the new.

STEP FOUR

In With the New Revelations 21:5 5 Then He who sat on the throne said, "Behold, I make all things new." And He said to me, "Write, for these words are true and faithful."

Before we get into this step, let's reiterate a point that we used at the close of step three. I remember lasting two, three and even four weeks without using drugs in the process of getting rid of the old me. Then, all of a sudden I realized something very important that I will note here. I will us an illustration to explain. At the time I was in my early 20s. So, imagine a 20 year old standing outside of your door with a ski mask on wearing a black hoodie. He's hiding behind the bush waiting for this 4 week old "new you" to walk out of the house. As soon as you open the door and take one step out, he begins to attack and says, "You know what it is, punk!" Who is going to win this fight? More than likely, this is an easy win for the 20 year old. My point is that you have to constantly guard yourself against the old you. The old you knows your every move. The old you knows exactly when to attack. This is a very crucial step in this journey. In with the new is one of the greatest turning points, because it has to be viewed as a new beginning. It's like pouring dirty water out of a glass. Before you put clean water in, you have to clean and sanitize the glass to get a clean pure drink of water.

Now that we have made it clear to the old you that they are no longer welcome, you have a lot of time on your hands. The process of getting rid of the old you clears a lot of time and space in your day to day life. This is where real understanding has to come into play. Step one, "Make The Decision," is constant. In the Lord's Prayer it says, "Give us this day, our daily bread." The decision has to be made day by day. It's like a base that lays the foundation of the journey. Step two, "Find The Love" is also a constant. When we explore the depths of this word love, it takes us much deeper than the emotional aspect usually equated with love. In The Honorable Minister Louis Farrakhan's Study Guide 18 titled, "RISING ABOVE EMOTIONS INTO THE THINKING OF GOD" it reads, *"We must not narrow Love to an emotional reaction. But when we say, "God is Love," the word is is represented by the = symbol, then Love has to be complete, because God is not an emotion. All of His Attributes are embodied in the Creative Force we call Love; an intense like for something is only one of its manifestations."* Now, with all of this time on your hands after clearing out all of that space to welcome the new you, old bad habits have to be replaced with new good habits. There is a saying that it takes 21 days to break a bad habit. Drug addiction is a bad habit. BUT, WAIT! Before you start counting your days, know and understand that the act of using drugs is the manifestation or the end result of something that went wrong in the mind. Whether we were truly aware of this fact at the time really doesn't matter. What's important is that we know this to be the case while on this road to recovery. Being aware of the thoughts flowing through our minds is very important. Because you are familiar with the old you. You know the thinking of the old you. So, you must be able to stop that person at the door and not allow them in. So, these steps are like working out. You can't go to the gym and get you a good workout in and think, I did it. Then, expect to walk out of the gym lean and mean. Stop it! You already know that's not how it works. It's alright to count your days. Just know that every aspect or step in this process has to collectively work on you to experience a true forward motion. Starting the process is key. Because the journey of a thousand miles begins with the first step. But, you have to keep on stepping to get results. And, seeing results feeds the desire to continue. Of course, with working out you start to see muscles that you never knew existed. Or, you eventually see the fat start to trim away. However, in this journey you start feeling better about yourself. You start seeing a new glow in your countenance. You start feeling brand new. And, you grow to love the very feeling of the change taking place.

In with the new is like building blocks. It's like making a whole new person. Becoming new is literally establishing a whole new world for yourself. You become a student of your own journey. You begin learning more about yourself, because you really start to pay more attention to what you know and things you thought you knew. I remember being back in the church and going down the aisle for alter prayer. Guess what? I didn't know how to pray.

So, I was peeking out of my eyes and the brother next to me said, *"YEAH!"* So, I said, *"YEAH!"* The brother in front of me said,
"THANK YOU!" So, I said, *"THANK YOU!"* After prayer I went back to my seat, I was so confused. I really could not tell what had just taken place. They would say things like, *"I can do all things through Christ that strengthens me."* And, *"God is in me, with me, through me and for me. And, where God is there can be no imperfection."* I would repeat this stuff all of the time and still smoke the night away.

This brings me to that talk with my uncle Paul
Armstrong (God Rest His Soul). I read Romans 7 and we had the discussion that changed my life. In that scripture Apostle Paul said,

Romans 7:21 *"I find then a law that, when I would do good, evil is present with me.*

22   For I delight in the law of God after the inward man:

23   But I see another law in my members, warring against the law of my mind, and bringing me into the captivity of the law of sin which is in my members.

24   O wretched man that I am! Who shall deliver me from the body of this death? 25 I thank God through Jesus Christ our Lord. So then with the mind I myself serve the law of
God; but with the flesh the law of sin." I find it very interested that my uncle's name was Paul. However, Apostle Paul is pointing out the duality of man. He is pointing at our human nature that deals with the urges and appetites of the flesh. And, he is making us aware of the higher power housed in our

flesh: The Mind. This can be illustrated as the mind being imprisoned by the urges of the flesh. Paul is giving us the origin of the battle. This is where the war begins. This encounter put me in touch with my dual nature. It gave me an understanding of flesh and spirit. The whole idea of gaining knowledge of self, had become much clearer. I began to understand the mind as it relates to the body, and the body as it relates to the mind. This understanding gave me power. It became clear that the body was nothing but a series of urges and appetites that the mind has complete control over, once the power of the mind is understood. So, a new way of thinking is most important in this step. It's still a challenge. It's still a struggle. But, things are getting clear. The question becomes, what can you do with your time now that you are cleaning up your life? I'm a musician. And, being in the church, my mind was determined to work my way into the "musician's corner" in the church. So, I started singing in different choirs only to work my way over to the bass guitar. I attended just about every service there was to keep my mind in a better place. Once, they heard me play bass, I was locked in as a musician. That was a most pleasurable escape. Outside of church, I started writing lyrics and producing music. Sometimes they would allow us to express our

gifts during a part of service called, "Inspirational Expression." All of this fed into the new man that I was striving to become. These experiences also made me feel so much better about myself, and how my life could be used to positively affect others.

Learning the duality of self along with the power of suggestion, gave clarity to what Reverend Wilson meant when he said, *"Pray as if everything depends on God. And, work as if everything depends on you."* It caused me to reflect on Genesis where dominion and power was given to man. Well, at least that's how I processed it. But, it all clicked one day. After struggling with being clean for a week. Back on drugs. Clean for 2 weeks. Back on drugs. Clean for a month. Back on drugs. I managed to make it to that magic number, for me, which was 90 days clean from drugs. I was laying down, smoking a cigarette listening to a cassette tape of The Honorable Minister Louis Farrakhan. He said something that I heard before. But, it was something about this time that set me in motion. He said, *"The body is the temple of God! And, you wonder why your prayers are not being answered. You pray to God and then you cloud your temple up with smoke....."* This was the last draw. I was already 90 days clean from the crack, weed, PCP, and alcohol. I put that cigarette out never to return to smoking, drinking or drugging again. In with the new. It all clicked. The beginning stage of a new mind began to form. A new mind is, in fact, a new man. I once heard the Minister say, **"There is nothing more powerful than a made up mind." Ephesians 4:23&24**

23   "and be renewed in the spirit of your mind,

24   and that you put on the new man which was created according to God, in true righteousness and holiness."

I will close this step with this story. Prior to this breakthrough, while in the process of deciding to make a change, the great Deacon Julius Jackson (God Rest His Soul) stood up and testified in front of the congregation. I had been up all night lacing PCP joints with crack cocaine. He said, *"It's been 15 years since I have drugged or drank!"* And, the congregation went crazy. While they were clapping and shouting, my mind started playing tricks on me. I looked up at Brother Jack and literally saw myself for a few seconds standing in his place. It felt so good, that when I snapped out of it, I said, *"I want to feel that again."* In my mind, that was my first time in a long time seeing myself off drugs. Now, some may read this and say that the hallucinogens that I smoked all night before church had me "tripping." That could very well be the case. But, I learned something of the power of the mind to realize what's imagined. The feeling was real. It reminds me of the study guided 18 that I mentioned earlier. The Honorable Minister Louis Farrakhan teaches where emotions come from. He states, **"The Brain is not only an organ** *of intellect and logic; it is also the source of Emotion. Emotions are brought to life in what is known as the limbic system. The limbic system is a collection of parts that constitute approximately 20% of the brain's area. The forces of pride, fear, joy, grief, anger, lust, hatred, envy, jealousy, arise from this region of the brain."* So, the feeling of joy over the thought of being 15 years clean was captured. And, just like that first hit of crack cocaine is the feeling that produces that never ending "chase," my mind was set to get that feeling of joy, in that moment, as a reality in my life. In with the new. Visualize the new person you are striving to become. Internalize how it feels *"as"* this new person. Act as if it has already taken place and embrace the feeling. However, do not get spooky. Know and understand that you are merely exercising your mind, heart and soul. This can be viewed as a mental and spiritual workout. Believe in yourself to accomplish the goal to become new, keeping the thought in mind that *"Mere belief accounts for nothing, except carried into practice."*

There is a lot that has transpired up to this point in the journey. Consider that there has been much deprogramming taking place, as well as, reprogramming. This means that there is so much information that you have discovered of yourself that you may not have viewed in the manner that you see things now.

It's almost like a big screenplay being played out on the big screen at the box office. The key is to know how to process what you are discovering. Good or bad, all data is to give us a better knowledge of how we are being developed to become what we intend to in this life. This brings us to the next step. Process the data.

STEP FIVE

Process the Data

We started out this journey by making a decision. Then, we realized that it was necessary to find the love. This new found love led us to the step of cleaning house. Out with the old you to bring in the new you. In these four steps there is a lot of data to process. There are a lot of new discoveries that require more of our attention, the more our minds become clear. This entire process is bringing us face to face with ourselves. To get the most out of this journey, the 5 W's must be explored - who, what, when, where and why. The knowledge in the 5 W's walk us into how to move forward in the right direction. In each section of this step we will start with a drill to put you in the mirror of truth. The objective is to go into the depths of your life, in past, present, and future tense. These drills do not have to be limited to the questions that are present. They are simply to get you started to move you into the depths of your own thinking. Let's explore these questions to get a clear picture of your thoughts to lead into a deeper look at "who."

Drill 1 - Who

Answer these questions with the thought of imagining your life in past, present and future tense.

Past

1. Who introduced you to drugs?
2. Who were they to you?
3. Who were some of the people you looked up to at that time in your life?

Present

4. Who are 5 people in your life the most?
5. Who of these 5 people have accomplishments in their lives that matches what you desire for your life?
6. Who do you admire at this stage in your life?

Future

7. Who are 5 people that have obtained the level of greatness you desire?

8. Who do you know that can get you to the level of greatness that you desire?

Who

There is a difference between who we are and who we've become. Think about it. We are born into this world. We live. Then, at some point we expire. From what I understand, our flesh is made up of the material of the earth. This material is not alive without the breath, mind and life force that's housed within. When we come into this world, we enter a place that we have not witnessed before. With this understanding, we begin learning from inside out. There is life in us. And, there is life outside of us. The journey begins. Everything that we see, hear, experience and are taught becomes data; our frame of reference. This is all that we have to bass life on.

Process the data. Who are you? There is so much information to consider when this question is asked. This writing is not designed to go in depth with this question. Rather, it is an attempt to encourage the reader to go as deep as you can within yourself to explore the question. Who are you? Typically, people define who they are based on what they do with the life that has been given to them. However, who might only have 3 letters, but it is a much bigger word. Who, in one since is used to question a person's character, position or authority. Who is also defined as, "what or which person or people." This definition speaks to the point earlier stated that, who we are is different from who we have become. In reality, often times who we are is more so who we have become as a result of circumstances and a lack of knowledge of our true selves. We will dig much deeper into this subject as we move through these steps. As for now, consider the fact that a deep study of this word is an endless journey on the road of self-discovery. We will find and redefine who we are all of the way through life, as it is a never ending walk towards our destiny. Think of it as playing a part in a movie. Here is the script. Now, your role in this movie is a drug addict. You study the script so that you can play your role to perfection. The reality is that you are not really a drug addict. You just have a role to play in this movie. Unfortunately, because of poor decisions we end up playing these type of roles in real life. This is what we mean by the fact that there is a difference between who we are verses who we've become. Because, in your and my essence is the reality of the God of Creation. But, we were born in a world of sin and shaped in iniquity.

Drill 2 – What

This next drill is designed to help to process the data toward becoming the new person that we talked about in the previous step. As you grow, things will change in your life. This process is different for each individual who takes these steps. Also, keep in mind that the more you grow the more some of these answer will evolve with you. Let's explore these questions to get a clear picture of your thoughts to lead into a deeper look at "what."

Answer these questions to get a clear picture of yourself at a very crucial time in your life's journey.

Past

1. What was the 1st drug that you used?
2. What was the reason you used it?
3. What was the effect it had on you?
4. What was your living condition at the time?
5. What stage were you in life? (child, teenager or adult)

Present

6. What's your age now?
7. What's your living condition now?

Future

8. What would you like your living condition to be?

9. What are you willing to do to get there?

This process will help you see what happened to you. It helps you to recall what condition you were in when you were introduced to that which you became addicted to. It's always good to know the past in order to not repeat the mistakes of the past.

What

What by definition is *"asking for information specifying something."* What? The more we explore who we are in our current situation, the more this word "what" becomes significant. Again, this is an attempt to chart out the course that I have been blessed to take in my walk to recovery. However, it's also my attempt to get the reader on the path of no return toward success. Once I began to discover who I am, I had to look at **what** took place to get me to who I had become; "A Drug Addict." It is very important to be true with yourself in order to get through this step. What you put in a computer is all that it has to work with to get out of it what you desire. So, face what it is that has gotten you to this place that you desire to overcome. The mind will process the lie and the truth and give you results. So, we might as well be truthful. The mirror of truth is the best place for change, analysis, awareness and judgement. I had to ask, "What are you looking at in the mirror? Be honest. Someone who abuse drugs. Are you pleased with what you see? Absolutely not. What would you like to see?" So, ask yourself these questions and be truthful and affirm your desire. When I got to this point in my journey, the answer to what I would like to see was a strong man free and clear of drug abuse moving on with my life to become a responsible man. What are you aware of that needs to change? Write it down and face it head on. My environment had to change. The type of company I kept had to change. I had to feed my mind with positive information, through reading and watching inspirational programs, just to name a few. Are you able to look at what you see in the mirror without having to lower your gaze? The answer to this question for me was no. And, that is something else that had to change.

What you are, verses what you have become, is worthy of deep study. Using myself as an example, it was very necessary to realize what happened to get me to this point. Ultimately, I made a choice to use drugs. As a result, I'm putting myself in danger and destroying my health. What are the possibilities? This will eventually kill me sooner than it would if I was not in this condition. These are a few points of reference to begin your fact finding mission on what got you to this place in your life. While you are exploring what took place, it will naturally lead you to when things started to go wrong. Let's explore these questions to get a clear picture of your thoughts to lead into a deeper look at "when."

Drill 3 – When

Answer these questions to explore your thinking to be able to further nurture the process of becoming a new person.

Past

1. When did you get comfortable with getting high?
2. When did you 1st realize that you had a problem?

Present

3. When did you decide that you needed help?
4. When did you honestly begin to seek help?
5. When did you start the process to make a change?

Future

6. When the change is manifest, you will know it!

This drill is designed to give a true account on when things went wrong. It's also designed to help get to the root of the problem by facing the mirror of truth. We have to be honest with ourselves and know that we have problems. In fact, when it gets down to it, we ultimately are the problem that must be solved.

When

When? This word is so powerful because it can get us to the root cause of our problems. When means *at what time?* When means *at or during the time that. When gets you to the bottom of your situation.* Reverend Wilson would teach that if a tree is in your way and you chop it down to the surface, it will one day be in your way again. Why? You have to go all the way down to the root to really get that tree out of your way once and for all. When for me was at 10 years old. This is when I first got introduced to smoking marijuana. I didn't know the significance of what was happening in my life at that time. But, it's a great point of reference to begin exploring that time and the conditions of the time. There is so much to consider. A couple of points to note are that we came up in a single parent home. My brother and I were raised by our mother. She did the best she could with what she had. She spent a lot of time working to keep food on the table. Not only that, furthering her education so that she could make more money to take care of her children gave us a lot of time to ourselves as children. She also spent a lot of time in church praying, in hopes that God would intervene and pick up the slack on her behalf where she may have fallen short. Her hardheaded sons would constantly make her late for service, because we really didn't want to go in the first place. So, at a certain point she got tired of wrestling with us every time she got ready to go to church. So, she began to start leaving us home. Needless to say, this gave us more time to ourselves to explore any and all possibilities that were presented to us to cut the fool. So, you have two young boys who are very energetic and adventurous. We have a lot of idle time on our hands. And, they say curiosity killed the cat. And, our curiosity was well intact for the cat, ya dig. There is a lot of information to process in this part of the journey. A main discovery here is that there is little to no logic reasoning in the mind of a 10 year old. Not only that. A 10 year old typically is not thinking about any long term effect on anything happening in their life as a child. Extract as much information as you can to get to the root cause of your situation. The more you study "who" and "what," it will take you pass the surface of your problem and get you to the root of when and "where" things went wrong. The next big word we will look at is where.

Before we get to the next drill, remember that the key to this step is to do the best you can to gain a thorough knowledge of yourself in the reality of your journey. We do not get a chance to go back and change anything. Always keep in mind that this step is meant for data processing. Everything that happens in our life has meaning. Every situation, good or bad, can assist us in life at this very moment. The key is to learn something from every aspect of the life that we are living. There is so much wealth that can be extracted from your life's story if you pay attention to the details. The steps in this book are just that; extractions from my life through drug addiction. And, because I have shared my story so many times in so many different ways, it was just a matter of time that these principles would eventually be laid out to help others along the way. Let's explore these questions to get a clear picture of your thoughts to lead into a deeper look at "where."

Drill 4 – Where?

Answer these questions to study your mental state of condition. The mind is where you find the power to change.

Wherever your mind tells you to go, that's exactly where you're going.

Past

1. **Where were you physically when you took your 1st hit?**
2. **Where were you mentally when you took your 1st hit?**

Present

3. **Where did it lead you?**
4. **Where are you physically and mentally now?**

Future

5. **Where would you like to be in life?**

This drill is designed not just to recall the space and time of your 1st hit. However, where were you physically and what was your mental state. Compare this with your physical and mental state today to see if there is a difference. Knowing where the addiction led to physically and mentally is very important, because it puts you in touch with your condition in real time. We also desire that this drill helps to instill in you a clear picture of where you would like this walk to recovery to take you. Know where you would like to be on the other side of drug abuse and claim it.

Where

Where means *in or to what place or position*. Where also means *the place or situation in which*. Where? Where are you today? Where are you going? What we discover in this study of self helps us to walk ourselves through the data that must be processed to help determine why we are in this place called drug abuse. Where were you when you took your first hit? This is a good time for a story. My cousin "*Moe*," who was 9 years old came over for the weekend. Moe, my brother "*Jr.*" and I who were 10 (me) and 11 (Jr.) years old were home alone. Moe pulled out a plastic sandwich bag and said, "*look at what I got.*" Me and Jr. replied, "*what's that?*" He said, "*I don't know. But, daddy be rolling it up and smoking it.*" This is where our journey began. We didn't know what we were doing. We didn't know where we were headed. But, this is real life. This is where our introduction to a way of life that had a lot of hills, mountains, pitfalls and stumbling blocks began. Study that time in your life when you took your first hit. Paint a clear picture of the conditions in your life at that time. This will help you understand a lot about yourself, then, to make the connection with how it effects your current state of condition. For instance, as I approached the point where change was inevitable, I was very irresponsible and idle. Yet, I was very energetic and curious to explore adventurously into the unknown depths of low life. So, explore where things are with you. Not the way you want things to be. Or, where you think you should be. Face the reality of your current state of condition. This is going to help you as you reflect on where it all got started. Because,

the information from then up to now will play a big part in helping you understand "*why*" you are in this position. I say this because, when I began to go through this process I realized that my decision making at 20 years old wasn't too different from my decision making at 10 years old. Being under the influence of drugs that long, can really have that kind of effect on the mind. You shall know the truth and the truth shall set you free. At this point it is time to answer a crucial question.
Why?

Drill 5 – Why?

This drill is designed to build logic reasoning in the mind. The mind is so powerful that once it is made up, there is no stopping you to accomplish what you desire. And, the mind is definitely created to think right. So, if your desire is to be right, feeding your mind with logic reasoning is a necessary exercise to develop that process. Note that if your reason is not strong and penetrating, then you're not ready. So spend time with these questions and make your answers to questions 3, 4, and 5 so strong that the thought of going against them will keep you up at night. Let's explore these questions to get a clear picture of your thoughts to lead into a deeper look at "why."

Answer these questions to reason with yourself. Also, answer these questions to exercise your mind towards the right way of thinking.

Past

1. **Why do you get high?**
2. **Why do you like getting high?**

Present

3. **Why is it necessary for you to stop getting high?**
4. **Why do you want to stop abusing drugs?**
5. **Why do you need to stop using drugs?**

Future

Results!!!!!!!!! The Future Is Now!!!!!!!!

Why

Why? Why *is the cause, reason, or purpose for which.* Why do we act the way we do? Why are we in the position we are in? Why should we even want to know why?

Everything in creation has a purpose. Every cause has an effect. When a human being looks deep into their lives there is so much information to process. Who, what, when, where and why is the pathway to reconnect with the source of life. It's the process of breaking the connection with that which hinders our way of thinking into a higher level of consciousness. There are so many things that can weigh down on humanity in this dog eat dog world. Especially those who have gotten caught up in drug addiction. In the walk towards recovery it is very necessary to feed the mind with positivity. The more I asked why, the more purpose opened up to me. I see more clear today, the purpose of my addiction. This book is a big reason I had to go through that aspect of my life. I had no idea then that this would be the case. However, the recall of all of the information that's in this book is clear evidence that my "Big Why" in life was housed in this seemingly dark and dreadful aspect of my life.

Why did we smoke that weed? First of all, Moe saw my Uncle Big Jr. smoke. His curiosity caused him to sneak some out of his father's stash and bring it to our place on one of his regular weekend visits. Now, when we use to go over to stay with them, my uncle was cool. He use to hang out with the fellas in the neighborhood while we were running around playing outside. Unk was our strength. He was the man in our life. He taught us many great life lessons. So, if it was alright for him, it must be alright for us. This is what we meant earlier about a little boy's logic. It's not that this is a conversation that we had. It's just how it all processed in my little mind, as I look back. Although, we knew instinctively that what we were doing was wrong, the mind is justifying the act because my uncle is cool. He's chilling with the homies in the neighborhood. And, he's teaching us great lessons in life. So, this can't do us too much harm, right. Wrong. Well, what's wrong? Something is wrong with the thinking. If we think wrong, the next step automatically is to do wrong. So, once we learn to think right, then naturally we can do right. Having the intelligence to ask why is a necessary component in understanding the purpose of a thing.

A true honest look at these 5 W's will help you chart out your coarse as to how you are going to win this battle.

Drill 6 – How

This drill is designed to exercise the power of the mind to imagine what you desire your condition to be and act as if it has already taken place. In doing so, the thought is to realize how it actually feel to achieve what you desire. Then, walk it down day by day and step by step to reach the goal. Let's explore these questions to get a clear picture of your thoughts to lead into a deeper look at "how." **Answer these questions to feed your mind with the uncompromising truth that will set you free.**

PRESENT AND FUTURE IS THE FOCUS!! THE PAST IS HISTORY!!

1. How do you feel being honest about your current situation?
2. How will you feed your desire to get on course with these steps to recovery?
3. How will you set yourself up to stay on course with these steps?
4. How, in your imagination, does it feel to be free and clean from drug addiction for 1 year, 2 years, 10 years. Close your eyes and go there in meditation for a minute.

The power is in the made up mind. The power is in what we accept. The power is in the decision. The power is in the love.

How

As you wholeheartedly process who, what, when, where and why in the mirror of truth, the method by which to help yourself up and out of your condition will unfold before your very eyes. How means *in what way or manner; by what means.* In the data processing period, know and understand that nothing happens without purpose. And, any and everything is designed to make you the person you are to become to fulfill a great purpose. Had I not gone through my experience with drugs, I would not be able to write this material. The way a drug addict is judged, you would never expect much good coming from them. In fact, the way an addict judge themselves is so detrimental that it becomes hard to believe there could be any great purpose for their lives. So, this work is a lift for the mind of the "addict" to never count yourself out of being a valuable asset to humanity. Everything that happens in our lives is designed to teach us more of ourselves to prepare us for a life of fulfillment. We are not always happy with what we have to face in life. However, the more we learn through the trials of life and even through triumph, the better we become as human beings. We endure through patience.

The study of who, what, when, where and why as laid out in this step speaks to how this whole project was produced. These 9 steps in motion were developed through the analysis of the 5 W's of my own journey. Who, what, when, where and why is comparable to "Man Know Thyself." It is the acceptance of the truth of self that helps to establish the principles and method by which to guide self to the destination of our desire. And, if we desire greatness, then how we get there is based on a thorough knowledge of self. So, through this process, you know who you are and now you can compare that with who you have become. You have a better idea of what to do and what not to do. You know when it's the old you casting suggestions, and you have the choice to respond or dismiss. You know where to go and where to stay away from, based on what you have discovered in this self-study. You know why good decision making is very important. And, there is nothing wrong with thinking things through to allow the feelings and emotions to drift away, so that you can make rational decisions. All of this lays the foundation of how to stay on track to continue to feed this new person that you are destined to become.

Let's take a closer look. In all of the information that you gather in this step in your study of who, what, when, where and why, you have a clear picture of where you are and how you got there. And, if you're reading this book for the sake of recovery, you know your desire to be clean. Now, in your everyday dealings you are more conscious of who and what you allow in your atmosphere. You also will have a better idea of when and where to go and where to stay away from. And, when you find yourself in the wrong place at the wrong time with the wrong people present, it becomes clear why you must dismiss yourself, immediately.

So, this step should help to keep your antennas up. The focus now is to do something great with this precious gift of life. The new you can begin to take charge of your steps toward greatness the more you nurture and develop that person who is destined to grow in and through your efforts to be great. The reference points in the "how to" is found in the details of who, what, when, where and why.

Surah (Noah) 71:13 reads,

"What is the matter with you that you hope not for greatness from Allah?"

YOU ARE IN THE FIGHT OF YOUR LIFE. DON'T GIVE UP!!! LET'S CONTINUE!!!

STEP SIX

Patience with the Process

Bob and weave! Stick and move! Plant and swing! Use the whole ring!

This step begins in this manner because the walk on the road to recovery is like a prize fight. The prize is freedom from self-destruction and self-abuse. The fight is internal. A good fighter studies the opponent to discover their strengths and weaknesses. This is what these steps are designed to do with oneself. The objective of the fighter is to establish a game plan to protect themselves from the strengths of the opponent and capitalize off of their weaknesses. If the opponent fights a consistent fight and the fighter sticks to the game plan, there is a good chance for victory. With this in mind, you should be the last person that you want to fight. Why? Because, you know all of your strengths and all of your weaknesses. Picture that.

The bell rings. You go center ring and look up to face your opponent, and it's you on the other side. That's and easy win. That's an easy knockout. You might as well throw in the towel. The point is that the more you beat yourself up, the more frustrated you become in striving to overcome the difficulty that you face. You don't want frustration to walk you into self-doubt. This can take you completely out of the fight. Understand this process as the battle of your life that you must win. Fight to win. Visualize yourself reaching the goal. Imagine how it feels and embrace the feeling. Imagine being free of drug addiction and being able to accomplish your goals and aspirations. Imagine having the lifestyle that you desire to live, free and clear of drug abuse. Have a strong desire, knowing that desire feeds the will. All of this takes extreme patience.

Having patience with the process is so important. When I saw Deacon Jackson say that he had 15 years clean under his belt and I had the nerve to see myself in his place, the journey seemed so far away.

And, when the decision is made to start the journey with determination, all it takes is one little setback to take you down. Question? If you were walking down the street and for whatever the reason, you trip and fall. What is going to be your first reaction? If you are not severely hurt, you're probably going to get right back up and keep it moving. Most people are not going to just sit there pondering on the steps they took and where they went wrong. You're not going to sit there in the middle of the street and beat yourself up about how you ended up on the ground. Get up! Stay in motion.

Here is a lesson on patience. At 12 years old, I desired to learn how to play the bass guitar. My mother purchased me a bass, a little amplifier and a 45 record that taught me how to tune the bass and it gave me the notes of each open string. That was as much as I was going to get. There was no time or money to pay for any lessons to be running back and forth to. It was so frustrating to get my left and right hand to coordinate. My left hand would be pressing down on the A string while my right hand was pulling on the E string. Or, I would pull on the D string while my left hand was pressing down on the G string. This was driving me crazy, almost to tears on many occasions. To make matters even worst, the blisters that began to form on my fingers would hurt so bad that it would bring me to tears at times. However, I wanted to play that bass so bad that none of this mattered. I picked that bass up every day, until my hands got coordinated. My desire to play outweighed the pain of the blisters that developed on my fingers. In fact, the blisters hardened my fingers to the point that they became immune to the pain. Having patience with the process was key. The desire to see the end result was also key. It felt so good to get to each stage of my development. I got to the point where I was listening to songs and finding the bass notes one note at a time. Then, the progression was 3 and 4 notes at a time. Before it was all said and done, I was able to play whole songs right along with the record. Being patient with the process will lead to good results.

Here is a quick story. One of the things that my aunt Lurendy did for me after I confessed my condition to her is offered her undivided attention to allow me to express myself. First she said, *"I don't care what time of day it is. If you feel like you are about to do something call me."* At the time we both were working in downtown Washington DC. We would meet in the park on 14th and L Street just to talk about my progress. If I had slipped, she would not allow me to talk down on myself with pity. She would focus on the progress and remind me that her phone line was open even if it was 2 or 3 o'clock in the morning. If we likened this to a prize fight, this was like the corner between rounds. The corner sees what you don't see. Remember to stick to the game plan in order to win. Don't be so quick to beat yourself over the head because of a mistake, without ever boosting yourself over any progress. Focus on the best part of your journey. In fact, draw from your strengths. It's something about each step in the right direction that boosts your morale to continue. Count each step as a score that leads to the win.

The game is far from being over. However, each score leads to the ultimate win.

Patience with the process. Every win is praiseworthy. I've found after learning how to put as much energy in acknowledging yourself for making progress as you do in beating yourself down for making a mistake, it will help you to develop enough patience with yourself to win. Patience *is the capacity to accept delay.* Patience *is trouble or suffering without getting angry or upset. Keep your eyes on the goal.* You have entered into a process. Process- *a series of actions, motions, or operations leading to some results.* Process means *a series of changes that occur naturally.* In this writing there are a series of steps designed for forward motion. These steps are operating procedures that lead to results. In order for something to lead, it has to be followed. Steps toward recovery causes us to make changes from unnatural behavior in hopes to walk us into our very nature, which is to be upright human beings. Stay in motion. The universe is constantly moving. We are universal creatures. If we are not in motion, we are out of universal order. In the title of this writing we say, "9 Steps In Motion." Motion is *the action or process of moving or being moved.* So, let us reiterate that these steps are continuous. They have to become culture. Because, if we are in a never ending process to become all that we can become, then consistent motion forward is necessary. This is also why we use "walking' the road to recovery. Walking is a verb. This also implies that the journey is continuous action. We cannot get comfortable and complacent. Pace yourself and keep it moving.

Take a deep breath. If you're breathing you have a chance. This whole process has everything to do with the right mindset. If you are truly going through these steps, your mind is changing. I heard the Honorable Minister Louis Farrakhan say that there is nothing more powerful than a made up mind. Repetition is key. This is not a sprint. It's not even a marathon. This is real life. And, it does not stop until you take your last breath. Constantly reflect on the decision you made in step one. Remind yourself often of the love you found in step two. Acknowledge the old you for who you were and accept the fact that this was a necessary aspect of your life to make you who you are becoming. Accept and embrace the new you that has a greater destiny beyond your imagination. In your walk on this road to recovery consider that all of your data, good and bad, is to develop you to serve a purpose that only you can fulfill. So, you might as well be patient with the process and reap the rewards that each lesson gives.

Seek assistance through patience and prayer. This is hard except for the humble ones.

STEP SEVEN

Focus On Today

Yesterday is gone. Tomorrow is not promised. All you have is today. Every conscious moment we have is in a period of time called today. Something that I realized on the road to recovery is that your past can haunt you. You know that you would lie, steal and cheat to get that next hit. Written in every move that you have ever made to get that next hit is information that you have in your mind about yourself. At a certain time in your addiction it had become so easy to lie, cheat and steal. The addict will destroy every voice of reasoning internally and externally with ease to calm the mind, in anticipation of the next hit. This is why we have a step called, "Process the Data." That step helps to keep us focused on today. You cannot undo what took place yesterday. But, you can press the reset button by righting your wrongs. The Honorable Minister Louis Farrakhan gave the best process of re-establishing relationships on October 16, 1995 at the Million Man March.

The "8 Steps of Atonement."

1. Point out the wrong.
2. Acknowledge the wrong.
3. Confess the wrong.
4. Repent for the wrong.
5. Atone for the wrong.
6. Forgiveness
7. Reconciliation and Restoration.
8. Perfect Union

Yesterday is already written. If you revisit yesterday and are able to go through these 8 steps with those who you have lied to, stolen from or cheated to feed your addiction it will help you in the process of becoming the person you desire to be on this road to recovery.

Yesterday will have you stuck. Yesterday can weigh so heavy on your mind that you are not able to even realize that the person who did this is the old you. And, if you stay stuck in yesterday, then the old you remains alive, active and in control. And you'll miss the opportunity that today offers to introduce to the world the new you. The old you was limited by the demands of the urges and appetites of your addiction. Letting go of the old you opens the door to a new and brighter future with unlimited possibilities. What you know about yourself yesterday can become a ceiling that you place on your own expectations. It's just fear of the unknown. It is also fear in knowing of what you were capable of doing. But, it is false. That was not the "real you." As we learned earlier in this writing, who you are and who you've become are not the same. Free yourself from yesterday because yesterday will be no more. This does not excuse your errant behavior of the past. And, to excuse or deny it will ill effect your present. In fact, if you do not correct this behavior, the pain and the consequences will follow you in the present and in to future. A major way that you can put off that old self is to correct those wrongs as the new you. Don't put off for tomorrow what you can do today. If you have a thought to do something that must be done, do it today. So many people lay down at night, never to see tomorrow. Even if you live to see tomorrow, when it comes it's going to be called today. Today is all we have. Not only that. Today moves so fast that it can get away from us. Now is the time to take charge of your life. Now, moves even quicker than today. Now is gone. Now is gone again. Now is merely a moment in time. Now what are you going to do? Since today is all we ever have, how will we utilize the limited amount of time that we will exist on this earth? So, strive to make every moment count. In this walk on the road to recovery, it will help to discover purpose. When you believe that you have something meaningful to live for, you will always have something worthwhile to do each day. Today is the day to do what is in your heart to do. With the right focus, all things are possible.

By the grace and mercy of Allah, I am able to say that it has been 28 years since I have used illegal substances, cigarettes and alcohol. But, day one of the decision to stop was full of anxiety. It was full of fear of failure. It was not the first attempt at trying to go clean. I had to understand that trying has levels to it. Try- *is to make an attempt or effort to do something.* But, it can't just stop at an attempt. Hence, the old saying, "If at first you don't succeed, try, try again." Even if you make several attempts and still have not reached your goal, it doesn't mean you have failed. View each attempt as a rung on a latter. Each attempt has a lesson that enables you to take the next step towards your goal with more determination. Even if the latter is on Mount Everest, one step at a time will eventually get you to the top. It's like rounds in a fight. You may lose the first and second round. The third round could be a draw. Then, you come out of the corner in the fourth round ready to rumble. You score a knock down. Now, you have a 10-8 round under your belt. The goal is to answer the last bell to raise your hands in victory. So, make an attempt or effort. Then, make your efforts stronger each time. DO IT! Get it done. Here is a drill. Try to close your eyes. Hmmm. How did it go? Ok. Try to ball your right hand into a fist. Ah. How did that go? See, I discovered that when I use the word try, it is only to set myself up for failure, so that if I don't complete the task I can easily say, "I only said that I would try. I didn't guarantee." This is why we say there are levels in trying. Your successes in your attempts builds your momentum to the degree that your trying becomes doing. Everything written of in this writing is what I had to face. If you are counting your days, know and understand that all you ever have is today. In the Lord's Prayer it says, "Give us this day, our daily bread." It doesn't mention yesterday or tomorrow. Focus on today. Focus is *the center of interest or activity.* Focus is *the state or quality of having or producing clear visual definition.* Focus on today and see yourself clearly in the position and manner you desire.

STEP EIGHT

Know Where You're Going

This is a great time to really look within yourself to identify with where you would like to end up as a result of starting this walk to recovery. This step is like putting a 2000 piece puzzle together. It's nothing special about the number 2000. I was just reflecting on how I use to feel after emptying the box of a 2000 piece puzzle on the table. Where do I start? I don't know about you. But, the picture on the box was always where I started. It was something about having the picture of the end result in my head that eased my mind towards having to deal with all of the pieces on the table. Another key for me was to get as much of the boarder done as possible. For me, knowing that if the back of the piece was straight, then it had to be a part of the boarder. What's my point in all of this? Picture yourself in the position in life that you are striving for. For me, that was a drug free responsible family man. A drug free business man. A successful drug free musician and artist. And, much, much more. And, because I knew that I was coming out of a lifestyle of having daily habits of scheming and conniving to get the next hit, I had to replace that with better daily practices. This led to more reading and writing. I read books like, "**Mis-Education of the Negro," by Carter G. Woodson, and "Destruction of A Black Civilization," by Chancellor Williams.** I got my hands on books like, **"Fall of America," and "Our Saviour Has Arrived," by The Honorable Elijah Muhammad.** It also led to more studying the Word of God and applying biblical principles to my everyday life. These actions were like placing those boarder pieces of the puzzle around my everyday life, so that my focus could be the picture that was being created inside the boarder.

There was a time when walking out of my door meant that I was going to get high, have a drink or smoke a cigarette, sooner or later. It didn't matter what else was going to happen throughout the day. As long as before it was all said and done, one or all of the above took place at some point before the day ended, I was good. Using drugs had become culture. It had become my way of life. Speaking of culture, I'm a musician, and I love playing bass guitar even to this day. I played in local bands. And, I have to say that I was then and even now, pretty good at it. I also had dreams of being a professional basketball player. So, we played ball quite a bit growing up. On top of that, I had become so dependent on drugs that it felt like I couldn't live without them. I am pointing this out because I want you to know that if this is you, these steps are designed to help reshape your culture. And, in starting the process, you have to be able to vividly paint a picture in your mind of where you're going.

Plan your work and work your plan. This is key in always having somewhere to go and something to do. Chart out your journey. Picture yourself taking a walk to the corner store. One step at a time, you can see how that journey plays out. Why? Because, you know where you're going. Knowing where you're going is very important. When you know where you are going and are determined to get there, it is harder to be taken off course. This is very different from starting your day without aim and purpose. When you have made a clear decision that you were no longer going to be depending on drugs, and an old "friend" or get high partner calls you up and asks, *"What are you about to get into?"* And your answer is, *"Nothing much."* You could be in big trouble.

Even if they know you are on a mission to clean yourself up, just a friendly, *"Why don't you come roll with me real quick. I'm about to make a quick run to my mother's house."* You're not doing anything. Why not? You're Homie is not on the same mission that you're on. So, he may light a cigarette on the way. No problem. Then, he may stop at the liquor store and grab a little taste. And, for all you know, by the time he gets to his mother's house you realize that he's not going to see momma. He's going to grab a lil something from the dope man in momma's neighborhood. This is just a scenario to point at the very point in this step. Know where you're going and move in that direction. Because, there is always someone who has somewhere for you to go that may not be the place you desire. So, have somewhere to go. This new person that you are becoming must be comfortable with establishing new spheres of influence. Have somewhere to go and know where you're going. There is nothing wrong with meeting people who have what you desire. They may be willing to teach you how they were able to accomplish their achievements. Beyond kicking the habit, begin to set short term and long term goals. This will assure that you have somewhere to go, and that you know where you're going. For instance, my brother and I planned to start a music project that was going to take so many hours of studio time. So, a goal for me was to save my portion of the money for each studio session. It felt so good to have my portion of the money each time we had a session. I also wanted my own vehicle. So, I saved up my money and purchased a 1977 Maverick. It was an old car. But, it belonged to me. And, that felt great. So, get some wins under your belt. It will definitely feed the direction you're going in.

It's something about setting a goal and reaching it that's so fulfilling. This builds confidence. One of the things a person coming out of drug addiction need is confidence. Confidence means *a feeling of self-assurance arising from one's appreciation of one's own abilities and qualities.* In knowing where you're going, to believe in yourself is key. However, the Holy Qur'an teaches that mere belief accounts for nothing except carried into practice. When you set a goal and believe that you can achieve the goal, this is the beginning of the process. It's sort of like the baptism we talked about earlier. Getting dipped in the water is only the beginning of the journey. The proof to oneself is in the practice and the obtaining of results.

We are almost where we want to be. I have another point to make about knowing where you're going. This book was in my mind over ten years ago. When I started it had a different title. The title was, *My*

Journey Through Addiction." It had steps involved. But, I clearly was not ready to write a book on this subject because I did not have a clear vision of how to lay out the steps. What I mean is that I was so caught up in day to day life, I could not focus on how to provide this information in a way to be a help to the reader. Life is still a struggle. However, I have just been blessed to dig deep into the purpose of this material to present it in a way to give insight based on practical application. As this project materialized in my head, the picture of how to lay it out became crystal clear in my mind. And, step by step here it is for you to participate in the process.

I was recently asked, "When you stopped using drugs, how did you get rid of the craving?" I had to stop and think. This is someone who I obviously had shared my story with. This was also someone who I worked with, who is very gifted in her culinary skills. I knew that I had to really concentrate on how I would answer this question. I simply started going through these steps that were already laid out in my mind. I have told many of these stories in this writing so many times. I have made these points on so many different occasions. So, I talked to her about making the decision. I went into finding the love. We passionately began talking about getting rid of the old you and making sure you fill the void, by creating and developing a new you. We talked about the drugs appeal to the pleasure center. So, we mentioned the fact that when you start filling in the time slots that we would use for drugs, it had to be with something pleasurable. However, not detrimental. You see, it came out so easy and passionately that it was therapeutic for me. I knew then that this is where I was going. I knew then that it was time to write this book. This work came through me so fast, it blew my mind. It reminds me of a word from my great Brother Milton D. Muhammad (Allah Rest his soul). He said, "Brother, every answer to your prayers come through people, places or things. And, time and condition will determine how soon you receive." So, know where you're going and pay attention to the people, places and things that you come into contact with.

Because, you'll never know when you'll be in the midst of the answer to your prayers. Know where you're going. Don't stop until you get there.

STEP NINE

Stay Relevant

Relevant means *appropriate to the current time, period, or circumstances of contemporary interest.* While earnestly striving to go through these steps, it is very important to embrace the mindset that you are relevant. You have to know that you are here for a reason. The fact that I am able to share my testimony with you in this book means that even at my worst state of addiction, at the lowest and most despicable point of my life, there was a purpose. Of course, I didn't realize it at the time. And, I'm sure that's the case for you. But, it speaks to the fact that your purpose is bigger than you. Everything in the universe was divinely created with a purpose. The fact that you exist means that you are here to fulfill a purpose that was divinely ordered. For this reason, know that you are relevant.

Stay relevant. Stay- *remain in a specified state or position. Remain appropriate to the current time.* Hold your position in feeding humanity with a high moral standard in a time where famine and pestilence is overcoming the world. This is the attitude taken in documenting this journey. Of course there is so much more that can be said about this journey. There are so many more stories of the ups and downs that I had to face in this walk. But, we just wanted to lay out principles and steps that could be understood and use by anyone reading this writing. The desire is to take my real life experience, and use it to serve Allah and serve humanity. In this way, I consider myself as making an attempt to be relevant. It is my prayer that whoever is struggling with drug abuse or any other addiction, and reads this writing is able to walk up this road to a successful recovery. Not for me to receive any vain glory. But, only to give all praise to the Most High for blessing us to share this information.

The more your mind becomes clear, the more relevant you become to yourself.

Throughout these steps the focus has been on the mind and in the mirror. And, everything outside of the mind and the mirror has a role to play in this journey as well. However, the mind is the focus. Because, the mind is in control. The body will do only what the mind suggests. So, by this time in the walk to recovery, the knowledge that you have gained about yourself will aid you in the process of being relevant. Your purpose has its own fingerprint. There is a specific reason that God had in mind when he willed you into existence. So, a key aspect in the journey to recovery is aligning your mind with your Creator to discover what He intends for your life. The more that you do this, the more you will see the Hand of God in your life. He was there all of the time, intervening in your affairs and gently guiding you along the way.

Like never before, the time and condition requires that we make our lives meaningful, and bring them in accord with what God has intended. As this book is being written, the world is in a pandemic.

Famine is on the horizon. There seems to be a real force causing human beings to determine whether or not we are justifying our very existence. It's either that, or we are just living life totally oblivious to a universal shaking and awakening to the law of cause and effect. This law has always been in effect. It just seems to be working at a higher rate of speed than it has throughout the generations, in my opinion. Time and circumstances have put me in touch with the importance of bringing this information from my heart and mind to the pages of this book, in hopes that it will help me to maintain relevance in such a critical time. Our journey together through this book contributes to each of our relevance. Through this book, the Creator has connected us in the path of this struggle to show forth His power to work through human beings to bring about positive change. By grace, this lines us up with the universal change that's taking place, and eternal purposefulness.

Congratulations! You have successfully gone through the "9 Steps In Motion" that have been laid out in this book. I pray that this information is internalized and practices on a daily consistent basis. The next chapter in this book is a brief summary, and a quick snapshot of my walk through the life that this book is born out of, up to this point in my life. However, let me draw a conclusion for this phase of the journey.

CONCLUSION

Prior to starting this book, my mindset has been on being relevant. I want to speak to you from the perspective that you are taking these steps seriously. There is a change taking place inside of you. Step two helps to develop a true sense of love for self in a rational, mathematical way. You know, 1+1=2. At this point I am not talking to a drug addict. In fact, if you understand this material correctly, I never was talking to a drug addict. By circumstances, we become other than ourselves. It's just a matter of time and under the right circumstances that we will realize that we have offered ourselves to the wickedness of this world. However, we are divine creatures who must now come up into the knowledge and power of our divinity. When we are able to do this we become relevant. The Creator, the Higher Power or whatever you choose to call this force is the contemporary interest. Humanity is clearly faced with circumstances never witnessed to this magnitude ever in history.

By the time you get to this point, I am concluding that you have a much clearer understanding of yourself. I am affirming that you have a better love for yourself. I am faithful that you are comfortable with making an attempt to move full-speed ahead, walking the road to recovery. I am praying that you are getting more comfortable with getting rid of the old you and welcoming the new you.

In all of this, the most important connection is the inward connection. This is the main focus of each step in this writing. Your first reading of this book may get you to a certain point in this process. You may have to read it again to get further along. Once the information in this book transfers from your head to your heart, you are well on your way. Most of what's in this book entered my mind, long before it entered my heart. It wasn't until it entered my heart that it began to work. The heart pumps the life blood. The brain is like the engine in your car. But, if you don't have fluid flowing through that engine, it's going to blow. I remember talking to a co-worker back in the day who felt comfortable telling me that she was struggling with crack addiction. At the time, I was struggling with crack myself. However, I had been back in the church for a while. And, I learned how to "say" some powerful things. So, I began to talk to her about some of the spiritual principles that are in this writing. A few weeks later, she thanked me. I'm wondering, for what? She said, "Through those talks that you have been giving me, I have not smoked crack in two weeks." I was happy for her. And, in my mind I said, "Well damn. I've been smoking crack ever since I've been ministering to her." The knowledge was in my head. But, it had not transferred to my heart. The information went straight to her heart, and benefited her. The time is now to embrace these steps so that it helps you. And, in your ability to connect with others, you can turn around and help someone else.

How many generations are you connected to? Are you in regular communication with the generation that came before you? I have found that typically when "older" people began to talk, the young begin to scatter. I, however, am usually one who would sit there and listen. I am fascinated by the stories of old. And, there are so many jewels in conversations with the elderly. What I have found in my experience is that regardless of their upbringing the elderly have a lot of useful information that can guide ones present walk in life. The same goes with the young. What's fascinating to me about communicating with the young is that often times, because everything is all new to them, they speak as if it's all new to you. This is where we have to be careful and skillful in our communication. How we respond to them can make or break the connection. Everyone wants to be validated. And, no one wants to talk to a "know it all." Here is the big one. What about the generation that you belong to?

When you walk into a room full of all of the above, is your presences welcomed? Or, do the all begin to scatter? Either is alright. Whether they welcome you or scatter, it gives you an opportunity to evaluate yourself to determine whether or not your approach to life is relevant to the time and circumstances of your surroundings.

Today is your day. The time is now. You know where you're going and you are grateful for another day and opportunity to reach your destination. Understand that showing gratitude is in what you do, not in what you say. Thank you for getting to this point in this writing. You are now "Walking the road to Recovery." And, you are going through "9 Steps in Motion." "Walking," because it never stops. "In Motion," because you must not quit.

TEN

My Walk with the Messiah (With The Mind
To Follow)

Let's take a walk. We came up in a household with a single mom raising to boys in the Washington DC Metropolitan area, affectionately known as the DMV today. My mother, Ms. Betty Jean Lea got us out of the city at an early age. We spent a lot of our time growing up in Suitland, Maryland. Mom worked real hard. In fact, most of her time was spent at work, church and adding to her skill set to bring in more cash to feed her family. She would drag me and my brother along with her to church seemingly every day. I am exaggerating. But, you know how it goes; choir rehearsal, Bible study, Super Salad Sunday, the church picnic, etc. It was always something going on at church. Needless to say, at a certain point, Ms. Betty got tired of wrestling with us, every time that she had to go to church. And, this is where the exploration process begins.

Remember, my little cousin introduced us to marijuana when he was 9 years old. After Moe snuck weed from his pops and introduced it to me and my brother, this started a journey that we had no idea of what was ahead of us. We didn't know what we were doing until one day *"Lil Darryl"* came over. Lil Darryl moved to the neighborhood from Northeast DC. He practically lived around the corner from a drug strip before his mom moved to our neighborhood. So, when he came over and saw what we were doing he said, "*Nope! You're doing it all wrong.*" We were rolling up weed in toilet paper. Picture that. Lil Darryl said, "*You need Top papers.*" He left and came back with some Tops. He sat at the table and began to teach. He was only 12 years old, mind you. He started picking the seeds out and said, "*These seed have to be taken out because they will start popping and making the joint go out. And, you will have to keep lighting it up*." Picture a 12 your old sticking the papers together, spreading the weed out in it, and rolling the joint up like a professional. Then, he wanted to see us light the joint. My brother lit the joint and Lil Darryl said, *"Nope, you have to pull on it."* He took it out of my brother's hand, pulled on it, choked and while still holding in the smoke, he said, *"That's how you hit the joint."* So, even though we had been smoking marijuana, we were not *"getting high"* until the "master teacher," Lil Darryl came and taught the lesson.

Our world was changing fast. There is so much that took place throughout the years as teenagers that this writing will not cover. But, it starts when Moe was 9 years old, I was 10 years old, my brother was 11 years old and Lil Darryl was 12. It didn't stop there. I am going to jump to when I was 19 years old. By then, I was not only smoking marijuana. I was drinking alcohol, smoking PCP, which we called *"love boat,"* I had been snorting cocaine, along with the biggest monster ever; I was smoking crack. I never thought that I would end up on crack because I had an encounter with it that scared the hell out of me. I had gone to New York on a crazy mission with another neighborhood friend who was like a brother, *"Ray Ray."* Now, Lil Darryl taught us how to smoke weed. But, Ray Ray taught us how to navigate through street life. Even though I was not *"from the streets,"* I learned how to maneuver through them from my brother Ray Ray. While in New York, we grabbed some pure cocaine that had been cooked down to *"rock"* form. We were in a hotel in Manhattan. I took a hit of it and the people on the television screen in that hotel room looked like they were in the room with us. I said to myself, *"I am never doing that again."* I few years later me and my homie *"Spoon"* were about to smoke some PCP and he suggested that we get some crack and lace the joint with crack. I met Spoon, Anthony Roy, in 1985. We were students at Lincoln Technical Institute in Capital Heights, Maryland. I said, *"NOOO, I'm not messing with that crack!"* He said, *"I'm telling you Mike, it's nothing like smoking crack. It's real smooth."* And, boy was he telling the truth. It was so smooth that it was a wrap. I WAS HOOKED. There are so many stories that I can share about my upbringing with the people mentioned so far. And, if I tell these stories in this book, it will be like an action packed movie on the big screen. However, we see enough of that already. In fact, this aspect of our community is glamourized and made so popular, that we tend to get stuck in a vicious cycle of self-destruction. And, my intent is to lay out principles that can help to break that cycle.

In this living hell, my late aunt Ann got me a job at 4000 Massachusetts Avenue in Northwest DC. I was a Porter in this high rise building.

One day while cleaning out the trash room, I saw the back of a book laying there on the floor to be thrown down the trash shoot. I picked it up and looked at the cover. Before I went to throw it down the trash shoot I read something like, "From Pimp, To Hoodlum, To Hustler, To Genius, Malcolm X." I was intrigued. I am around hoodlums, hustlers and pimps all day, every day. I was wondering how this dude became a genius. So, I took the book home and couldn't put it down.

I'm reading the autobiography of Malcolm X and it is blowing my mind. At 19, I had no idea who he was. I knew nothing of the black man's
contribution to civilization. I knew nothing about
The Most Honorable Elijah Muhammad, The
Honorable Minister Louis Farrakhan or The Nation of Islam. My mind was blown. The first reaction was anger. I became upset that all of this time had gone by and I had no idea of this very important information that would give me a greater sense of self. Something was happening with me. I was still on the block. I was still getting high. But, I was still reading the book. I was sitting on the steps one day on the drug strip reading. An older brother came out of his building on his way to work and asked, *"What's that you're reading young man?"* I showed him the cover and he said, *"You keep reading that and one day you're going to be dangerous."* Now the end of the book got real cloudy to me. I didn't understand the split between Brother Malcolm and the Nation. However, I was so fascinated my

language began to change. Even still, I was still trapped behind the bars of my own thinking, and hanging on that block.

One day on the strip. I was sitting on those same steps. A young brother who I had not seen around the way before called me into the building. I came to him and he showed me several bags of crack rocks. Each bag had ten $20 pieces in them. He asked, "*You want some work*?" My heart started beating real fast. I thought, "*Who is this*? *I don't sell drugs.*" *I abuse them.*" As nervous as I was I took him up on his offer only to immediately disappear. I got ghost so quick. And, unfortunately went home and smoked all ten of those crack rocks back to back. My heart was beating so fast. Not only because of all of the crack rocks that I smoked. But, at the same time my thoughts were, "*You're a dead man.*" This was the late 80s. DC was the "*Murder Capital*" of the country at that time. And, I knew of people who were taken out for way less during those days.

I didn't know this young brother at all. If I saw him today, I would not even be able to identify him. One could say, he was an angel. Because, I was so afraid to go anywhere near that block again. I knew there would be no questions asked. So, where do I go? What do I do?

Life as I knew it was changing fast. Around this time the Fruit of Islam in Washington DC had started going into the worst drug areas to help clean up the neighborhoods. I was attracted to the Nation of Islam. However, with the misunderstanding of the end of the autobiography of Malcolm X along with the work the FOI were doing in the community, I was afraid to go straight to the mosque. So, I did the next best thing and went back to church. My thoughts were to go and clean my life up a little before I go over to the Nation. I spent six years back in church growing spiritually. I spent six years under the leadership of Pastor Willie F. Wilson. Under this great teacher, I was blessed to get rid of the drugs, alcohol and cigarettes by getting involved and going through these steps highlighted in this book. The whole time I had been asking Allah, "*Is it time to go to the mosque?*"

I am going to touch an area in my journey real quick. In the fourth step, "*In With the New*," we talked about all of the time we would have on our hands after making a real decision to go clean. We also talked in this writing that illegal drugs are designed to appeal to the pleasure center. A great problem arose in my journey. During that time, after drugs and alcohol were no long my vices, sex had become a major escape and my new drug of choice. Because of the danger of this disposition, it had become very clear to me that it was time for the military structure of the Fruit of Islam that is found in the Ranks of the Nation of Islam.

Before we look at how I made my transition into the Nation, I want to share a moment in this journey that highlights a brotherly connection that took place between myself and one of the associate Minister's in Union Temple. I remember being terminated from my job at FDIC. Everyone looked at me as "*Militant Mike*," so most people asked, "*What did you do this time?*"

Or, why did they get rid of you?" The energy and spirit was along the lines of assuring that I had it coming. But, the first thing that Minister Eric Kareem asked was, *"What can I do to help you brother?"* We established a strong bond of brotherhood. In fact, it was through Brother Kareem that I branched out on my own for the first time as an adult. We share a place together. And, I got the experience of paying my own bills. The beauty of this brotherhood was that Brother Kareem had so many video tapes of the Honorable Minister Louis Farrakhan. I would soak in the words from those lectures on a regular basis. Our bond became real strong. We bumped heads on occasions. And, because we both were ball players. We never thought to go to blows. We said, *"Let's take it to the court."* And, we would go to the gym and knock each other around in a few one on ones. Kareem gave his little brother a good spanking out there. But, we left the court tighter than we were before we left our place, going at each other. Leading up to our *"Men's Day"* service on September 19, 1993, where the keynote speaker was The Honorable

Minister Louis Farrakhan there were rumors spreading in the church that I was leaving the church for this reason, or that reason. The reasons that were spreading are not important. The fact that there were rumors is what I felt a need to address. So, I sat with Pastor Wilson as a spiritual son and let him know, *"As any father would like to see that their son could leave the house and make what he has taught a reality, this is a necessary step for me to move to the next phase of discipline in my life."* He understood and blessed my decision.

The Honorable Minister Louis Farrakhan spoke. It was powerful as usual. I played bass for the Men's Day Choir and I was in my zone. After service, the Minister went downstairs to the fellowship hall to shake hands with those who would like to greet him. I stood in that long line wondering what I would say. By the time I came face to face with the Minister, we exchanged the greetings and shook hands. Before I could say anything he said, *"Bass player right?"* I said, *"Yes sir."* He said, *"You know, you play a good bass."* I was blown away that he would acknowledge me when I was trying to figure out what to say to him. The only thing I could think to say afterwards was, "*Thank you for showing me what a free man looks like. I hope to be that way one day.*" He looked me through my eyes down into my soul and said, "*Don't worry brother. You will.*" This was the preface of my walk with the Messiah. My journey into the Ranks of the Nation of Islam was about to begin.

The next day, Monday September 20, 1993 I was in processing class of the FOI at Muhammad Mosque #4 at 1615 Kenilworth Avenue NE DC. My journey walking with the Messiah began. I say walking with the Messiah with the mind to follow. Walking with the Messiah is a stage of development. In this stage we are striving to make our word bond. We are in a process of discovery. This process is to walk us into becoming one with our God. There is a difference between walking with and following. Our desire is to become a true follower by totally shedding myself of the darkness of this world and fully living the life of one totally submitting my will to do the Will of God.

This part of my journey is full. It would take several books to touch this aspect of my life. So, I will just touch a few moments of significance that speaks to the subject matter of this writing. The first thing is my introduction to the Final Call Newspaper Program. After about 4 weeks in processing class my Lieutenant at the time Brother Lt. Hassan Muhammad pulled me to the side after class and handed me 25 Final Call Newspapers and said, *"I want you to soldier these papers."* I was excited and nervous at the same time. It was cold outside. I was brand new to this process. And, I knew that people were going to test and try me with information that I would not be able to address. I challenged my fears and made it through. That was on a Saturday. I couldn't wait to get to the mosque to give this money to Brother Hassan. I saw him and gave him the money. Because of the time, we had to get situated for the meeting. After the meeting Brother Hassan came up to me and gave me back some of the money. He said, *"You know you keep 30%."* I was lit. See, growing up, we were always attracted to the drug dealers. My problem with that is that I broke all of the rules. And, instead of making money, I smoked up everything that I could get my hands on. But, this got me excited because I knew that I could finally build myself up to do for self. Any of you who know me knows that the block became my way of life. The beauty of this is that the same principle of "*hanging around*" until the mission was accomplished in the world of addiction became a great discipline in the world of doing for self. As a drug addict, the determination, dedication, consistency and drive to get the next hit had become identical to the desire to be successful each day in reaching my daily goals "pushing the program." So, the same principles that were taking me down and out of life, used properly, are the very principles that feeds the heart mind and soul for success, on the other side of the equation.

The next point I would like to make about this journey is my marriage. We are taught that marriage is half of our faith. One of the best things that has taken place in my life in my walk with the Messiah is my marriage to Sister Nneka Muhammad. Why is this significant for this writing? The Holy Qur'an teaches that men are the maintainers of women. This is a great responsibility. It tests the fiber of your being to maintain a woman physically, spiritually, emotionally, psychologically, intellectually and economically. It is a major challenge to strive to become one with another human being. Accepting the challenge puts us on a course to become "*followers*" of the Messiah. This, in turn, puts us on track to become one with Allah(God). In a counseling session with our Student Mid-Atlantic Regional Minister Abdul Khadir Muhammad he said a lot that speaks to the mindset that must be developed as a man and husband. For instance, Brother Khadir said, "*We are taught that what's yours is hers. And, what's hers is hers.*" This helps to shape the mind of a maintainer. When you enter into marriage with this mindset, it forces the mind to elevate to take on the task. He asked my court mate at the time, "*What do your feet hit each morning when you wake up*?" She confusingly said, "*Carpet*?" He looked back towards me and said, "*You hear that Brother? She shouldn't have anything less! You have to be willing to shovel dog mess to take care of our Sister.*" This was such a great encounter. It set my mind to stay determined to weather any storm. The whole process and journey of marriage helps to keep the mind straight.

The Honorable Minister Louis Farrakhan teaches that "*A Nation Can Rise No Higher Than It's Woman.*" He also has a lecture titled, "*How to give birth to a God.*" That's the other part about marriage that makes my life in this journey so rewarding. The fact that my wife is "**ALL IN**" when it comes to her MGT G.C.C. (Muslim Girls Training & Civilization Class), when it was time to give birth, the thought of giving birth to a god was foremost in her mind. And, because she was free to be Muslim. Free to be a wife. Free to be a mother. She raised our daughter as a citizen of the Nation of Islam. Our daughter, Tasnim Muhammad was either homeschooled or in one of our schools in the NOI up until college. She graduated high school at 16 years old as valedictorian. At, 19 years old, Sister Tasnim is in her senior year in college. She has been an honor student all of her life. This is encouragement for the reader who may have gotten caught up into drug addiction, who thinks nothing good can come from their loins. By the grace of Almighty Allah, never count yourself out. Your life is not over until you take your last breath. And, depending on how you live your life while on this earth will determine whether you live beyond the grave. I am not talking about in the great by and by in the sky. But, how will you be remembered? Or, will you be forgotten? Drop dead, and then your life stops? No! No! No! Leave a lasting impression on those who cross your path.

The last thing that I want to point out in my walk with the Messiah is this. When I stated to the Minister that I hoped to one day be free and he assured me that I would, I had no idea that I would one day relocate to our headquarters, here in Chicago. Well, here we are, in Chicago. Because of the desire to be free, regardless of what job I landed, I always ended up back on the block. It always was a struggle. But, there always was a level of peace within as well. It reminds me of the late soldier Brother Maurice 2X, who had become Brother Maurice Muhammad. (May Allah be pleased) Early in my block days, he came up to me and said, *"Brother Michael, you don't want to do this for 10 years. My feet hurt Brother Michael."* I knew what he was saying. But, he was stuck on the block himself and did not know how to guide me. I love him forever for planting that seed in me. Needless to say, I ended up on the block for 20 years. However, I learned how to make one of the best bean pies in the country and, by Allah's Grace, my work ethics and determination have been noticed by many. I have to admit that this is another *"quality"* of the addict. An addict's work ethic when it comes to getting that next hit is impeccable.

Before I left the DMV, one of the closest brothers that I have been able to establish a bond with, Brother Raymond L. Muhammad said to me, *"It's going to be a lot of people watching you Brother Michael."* Let me explain something. Brother Raymond likes to keep things simple and straight to the point. However, everything he says has depth to it. While I am talking about Brother Raymond, I have to say that most of what I have been able to acquire as far as a mindset to do for self comes from my relationship with him. For the 26 plus years that I have known him, I have never known him to punch the clock for someone else. Not only that he has a wife and six children that he has been the sole provider for since I have known him. I also want to mention Brother Roger (2X) Muhammad. Brother Roger was the first Brother who made sure that I got a copy of my Supreme Wisdom Lessons. And, we use to pound the pavement for hours a day together to keep each other thinking properly to meet the goal. Back to the work ethic. The work ethic that I have been blessed to acquire in my day to day grind, along with the fact that we have a great product, was recognized by Sister Carmella Coqmard Muhammad. Sister Carmella was able to realize one of her desires to open a restaurant, and decided to invite us in. This new reality called, "The Foodie's Spot" became one of the great highlights of hope for believers across our Nation, as well as for the troubled community right across the street from Mosque Maryam. The community looks at The Foodie's Spot as a breath of fresh air. It's a much needed place where you can come and grab a good healthy and wholesome bite to eat. It is also the home of my brand, Paradise Desserts, LLC. And, it's the place that helped me to get off of the block. It is also a great part of our efforts to realize this destination towards the freedom that we desire.

In my conclusion, I want to point out a few words of the Honorable Minister Louis Farrakhan to myself and Sister Carmella on his first visit to The Foodie's Spot. He stood in the doorway and said, "*As Salaam Alaikum.*" He sounded just like the Honorable Elijah Muhammad. He stepped into the doorway and looked to his right at Sister Carmella and said, "*Thank you for your courage Sister.*" Then, he looked across the room to me and said, "*Thank you for your courage brother.*" He took a few steps in and looked around and said, "*I feel good. I feel like you're going to be successful.*" Then, he looked out of the door across the street at Mosque Maryam and said, "*See, you don't have to wait for the mosque to do something like this!*" I point this out for everyone reading this writing. Step out on faith and do not wait for permission to do something courageous that would give hope to others on the fence contemplating on whether or not they are going to step out on faith.

First and foremost. If you have gotten to this point in this book, words are not adequate to say how grateful and thankful I am. I truly appreciate you. It has been very therapeutic for me to recall this information to put it all together. If you are struggling with addiction of any kind, I pray that you have the courage to go through these steps. I also pray that you are able to internalize the information in this little book, so that it will get you on this road with the understanding that it's a never ending journey. This is the beginning of a walk to oneness with Allah(God). This is a reference to a subject matter that cannot be exhausted. Because, this subject matter explores the depths of the mind. I thank Allah for using me to tell the story of this journey in hopes that it will feed the heart and mind of the reader to go deep enough into your mind, heart and soul to make the connection with the power of Allah(God) within to meet and overcome all obstacles in our path. May Allah bless us with the Light of Understanding.

As Salaam Alaikum

Made in the USA
Las Vegas, NV
31 January 2021

16847671R00066